RECORDED VERSIONS GUITAR

AUTHENTIC TRANSCRIPTIONS WITH NOTES AND TABLATURE

Transcribed By JESSE GRESS

STEVIE RAY VAUGHAN AND DOUBLE TROUBLE
SOUL TO SOUL

T0053166

ISBN 978-0-7935-4414-1

HAL•LEONARD® CORPORATION

7777 W. BLUEMOUND RD. P.O. BOX 13819 MILWAUKEE, WI 53213

February 1986 - Houston, Texas. Photo by Tracy Hart.

STEVIE RAY VAUGHAN AND DOUBLE TROUBLE
SOUL TO SOUL

May 4, 1990 - Austin, Texas. Photo by Tracy Hart.

January 31, 1987 - Houston, Texas. Photo by Tracy Hart.

November 24, 1989. Photo by Tracy Hart.

Jimmie and Stevie Ray Vaughan. February 1986 - Houston, Texas. Photo by Tracy Hart.

Say What!

By Stevie Ray Vaughan

Tune Down 1/2 Step:

① = Eb ④ = Db

② = Bb ⑤ = Ab

③ = Gb ⑥ = Eb

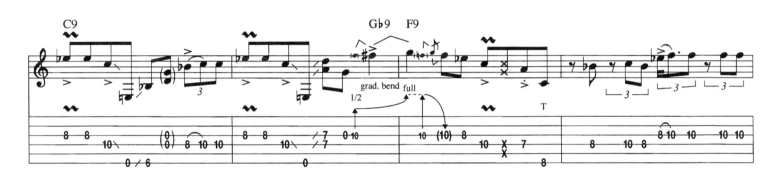

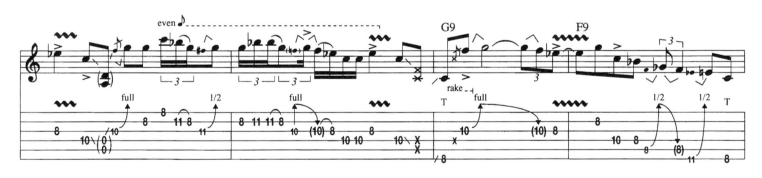

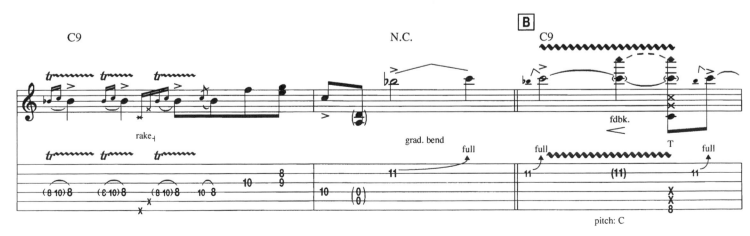

pitch: C

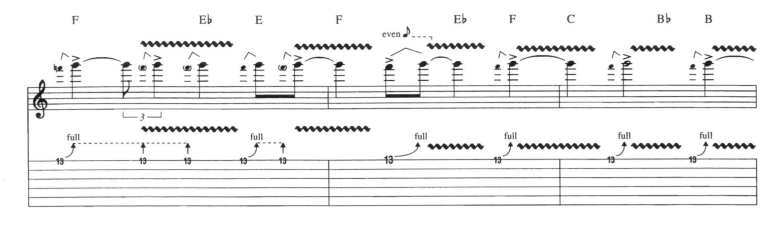

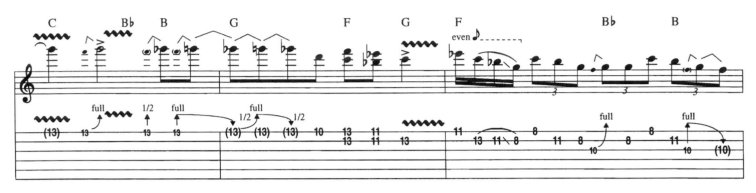

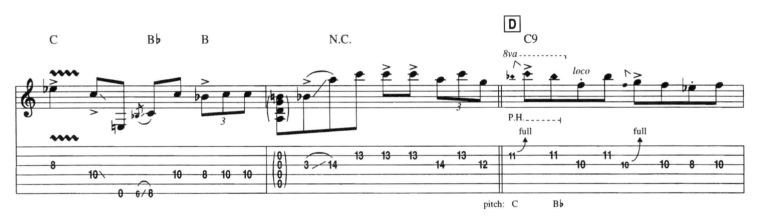

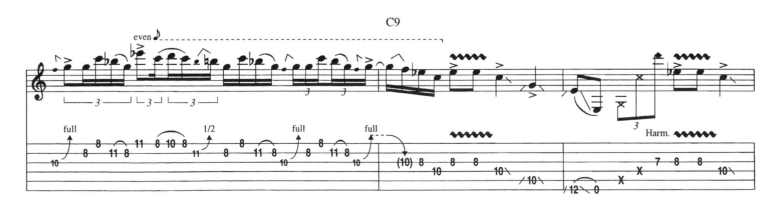

10

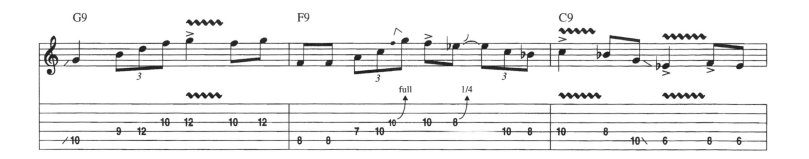

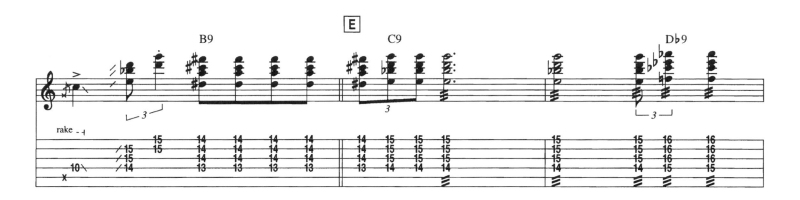

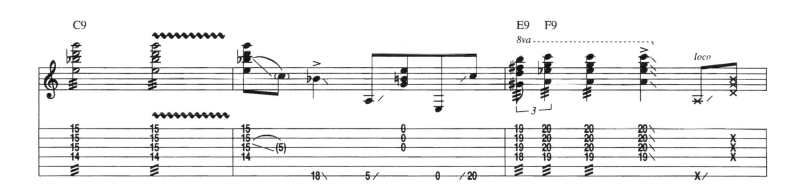

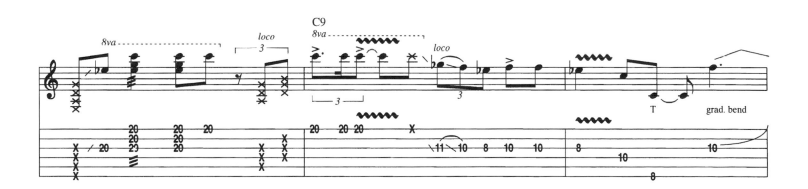

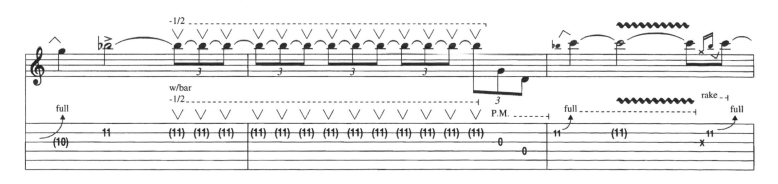

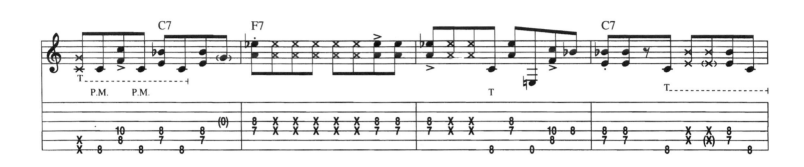

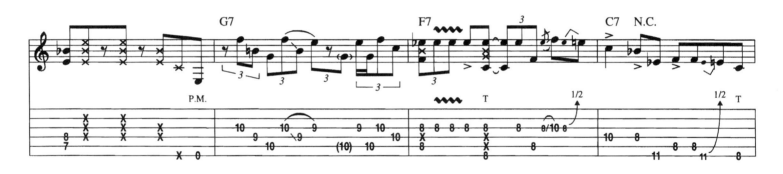

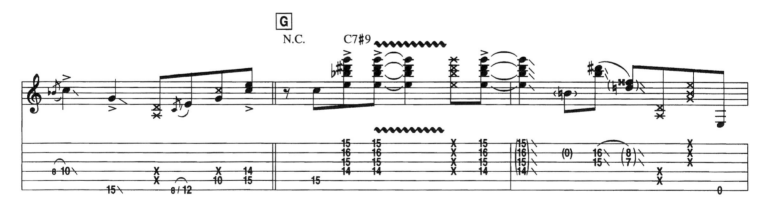

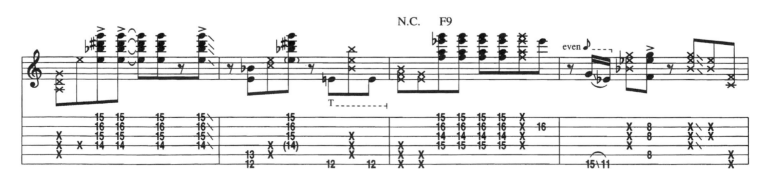

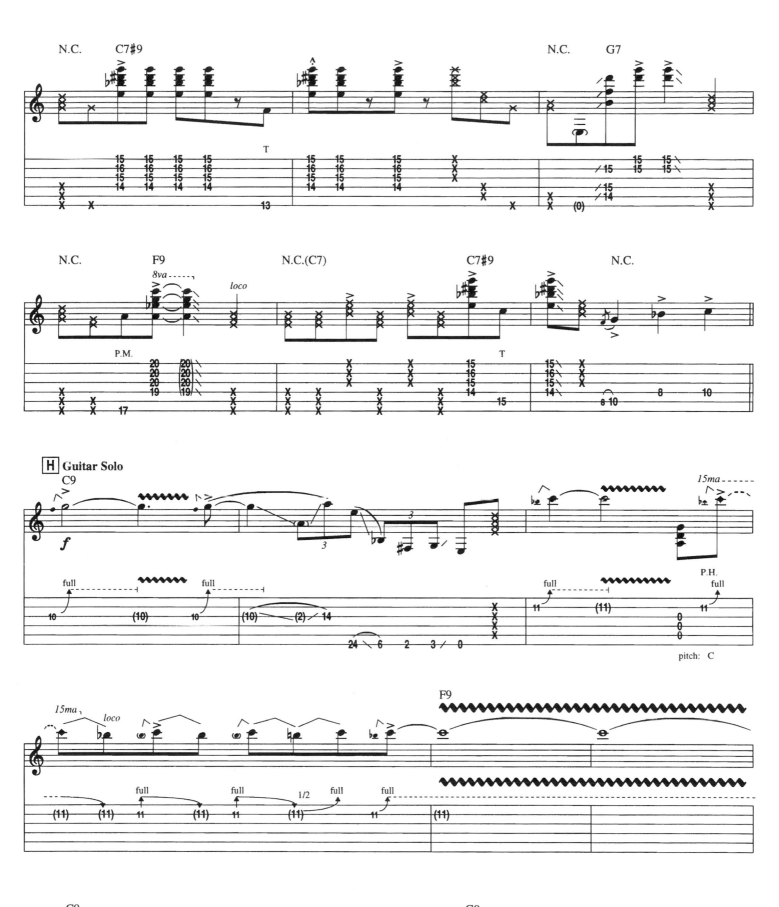

H Guitar Solo

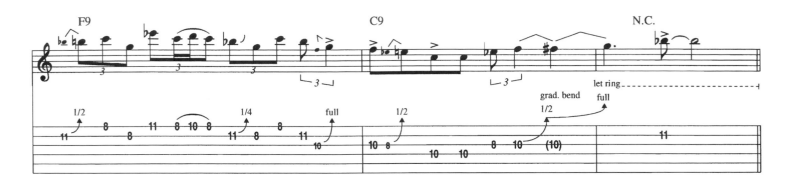

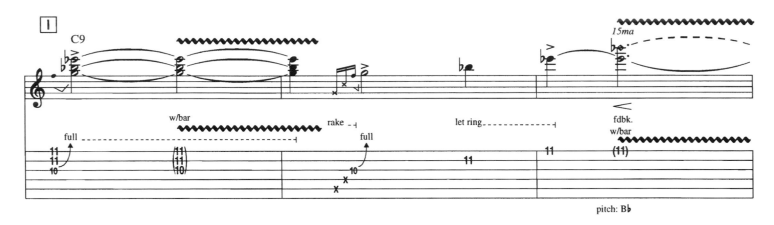

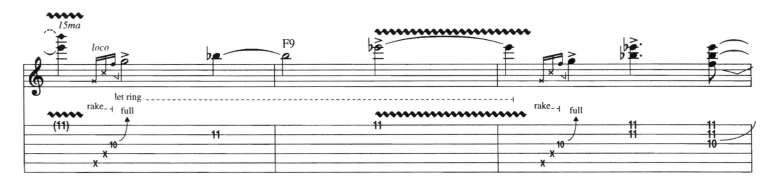

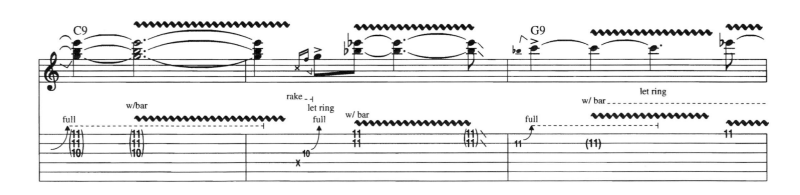

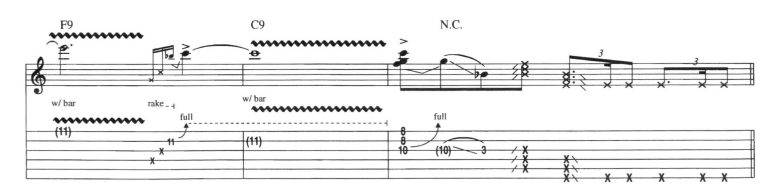

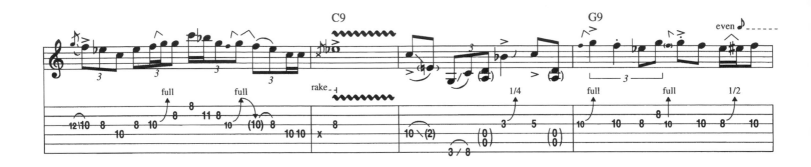

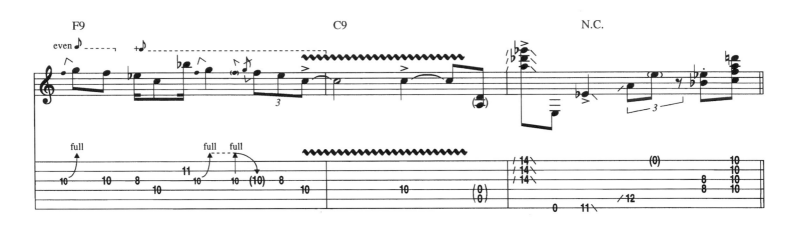

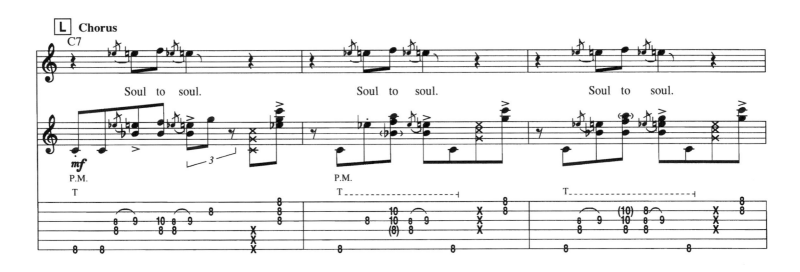

L **Chorus**

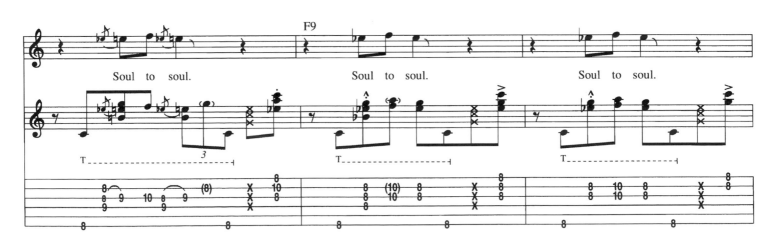

Soul to soul.

Soul to soul.

Soul to soul.

Soul to soul.

Soul to soul.

M Guitar Solo

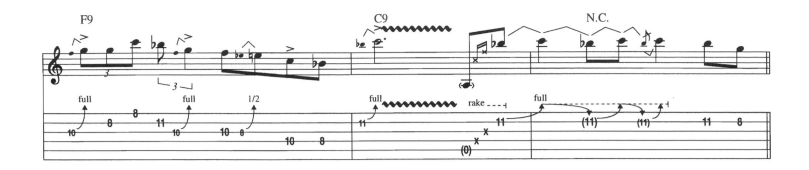

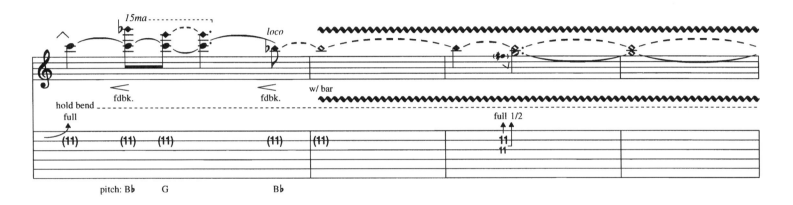

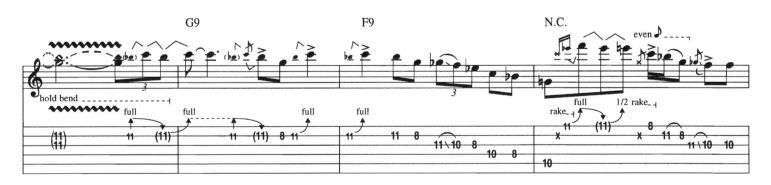

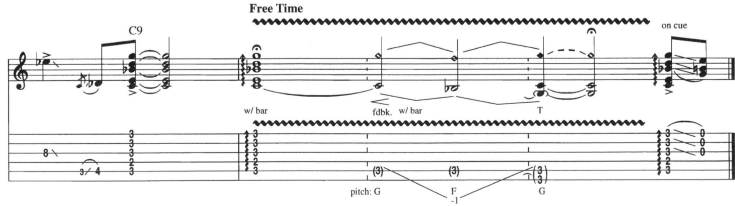

Lookin' Out The Window

By Doyle Bramhall

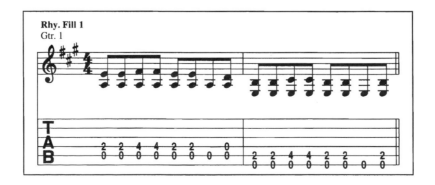

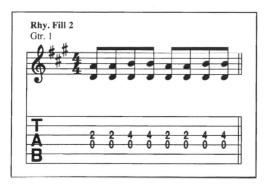

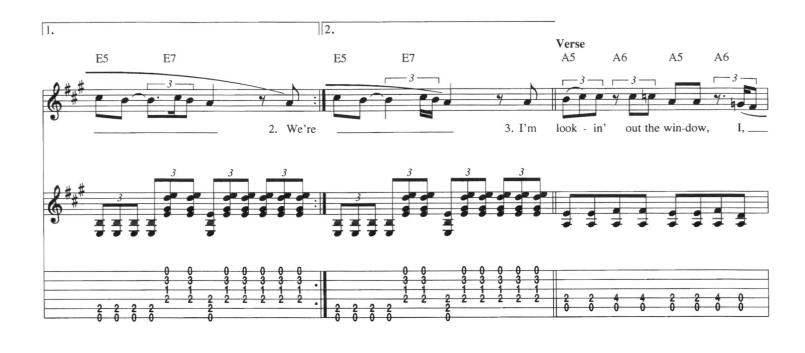

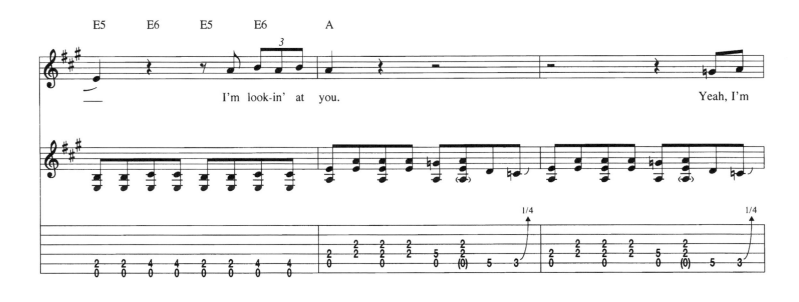

Look At Little Sister

By Hank Ballard

Tune Down 1/2 Step

①= Eb ④ = Db
②= Bb ⑤ = Ab
③= Gb ⑥ = Eb

Moderate Shuffle ♩ = 112

Triplet Feel (♫ = ♩♪)

Verse
*E

1. Hey, hey, hey, hey, hey, ma-ma, look at lit-tle sis out in the back-

Gtr. 1

mf

*Chord symbols reflect suggested tonality.

A7

- yard shak-ing like __ this. __ Hey, hey, hey, hey, hey, hey,

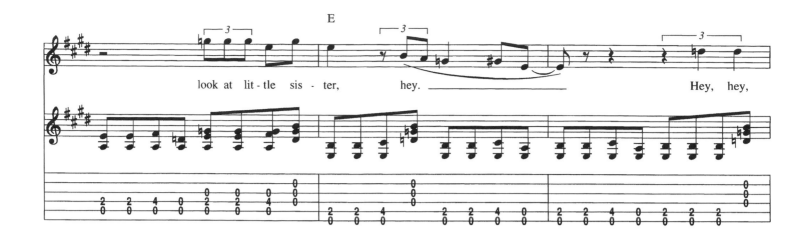

look at lit-tle sis-ter, hey. _____ Hey, hey,

*B7   A7   E

hey,   hey, __   look at lit-tle sis-ter.

*Bass plays B on this & all subsequent B7 chords.

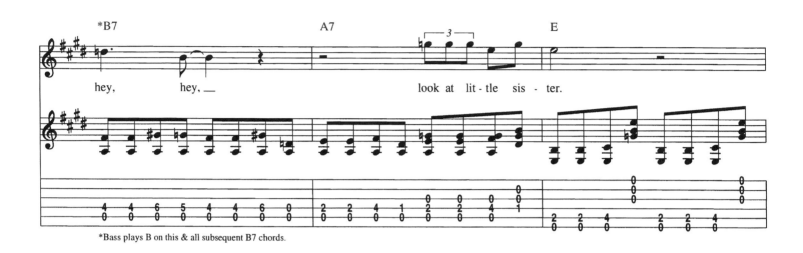

Verse

N.C.   E

2. What a-bout the neigh - bors,   what they gon-na say? _

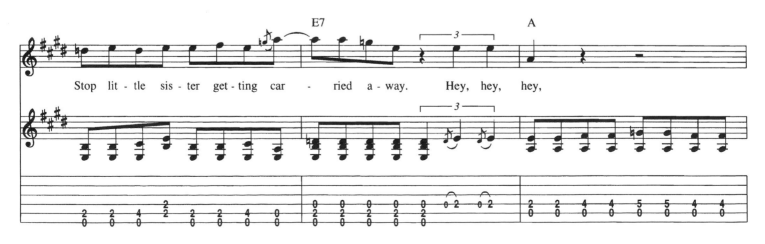

E7   A

Stop lit-tle sis-ter get-ting car - ried a-way.   Hey, hey, hey,

look at lit-tle sis-ter, hey. _____ Hey, hey,

hey, hey, _____ look at lit-tle sis-ter.

Verse

3. Shak-ing like a tree, _____ roll-ing like a log. _____

Shak-ing and a-roll-ing, now that ain't all. _____ Hey, hey, hey,

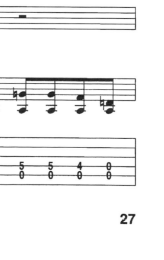

look at lit - tle sis - ter,   hey. _____   Hey, hey,

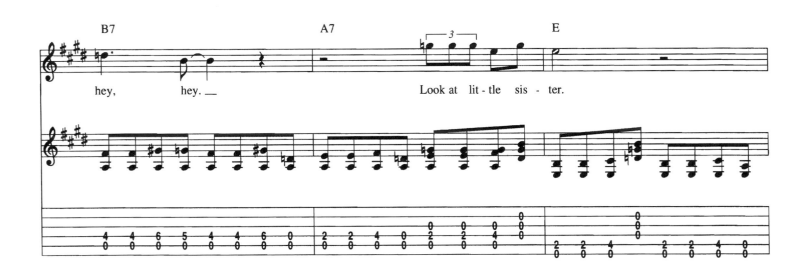

B7   A7   E

hey,   hey. _   Look at lit - tle sis - ter.

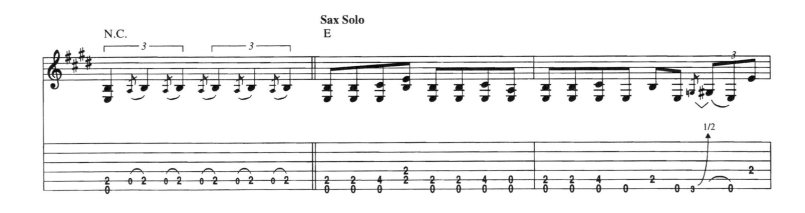

Sax Solo

N.C.   E

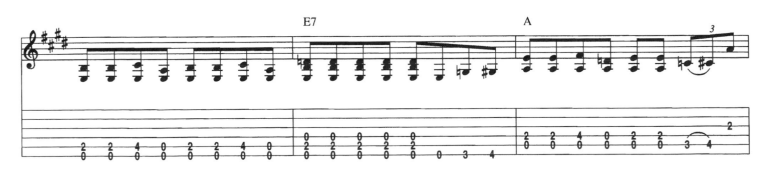

E7   A

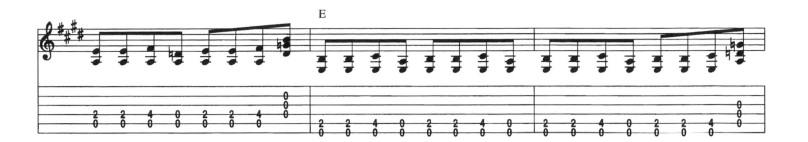

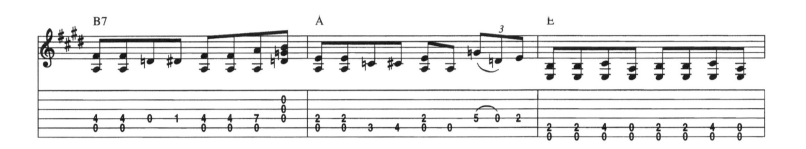

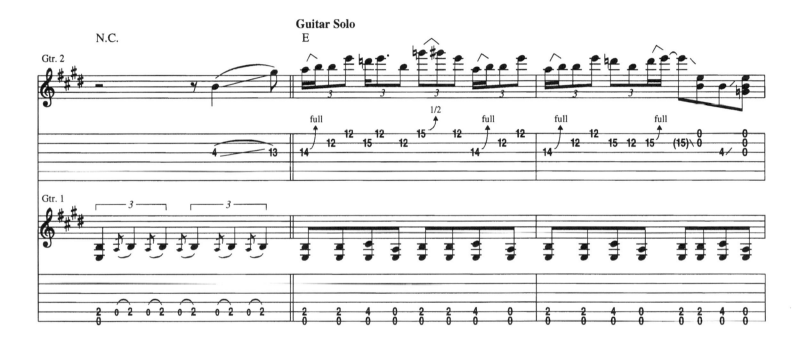

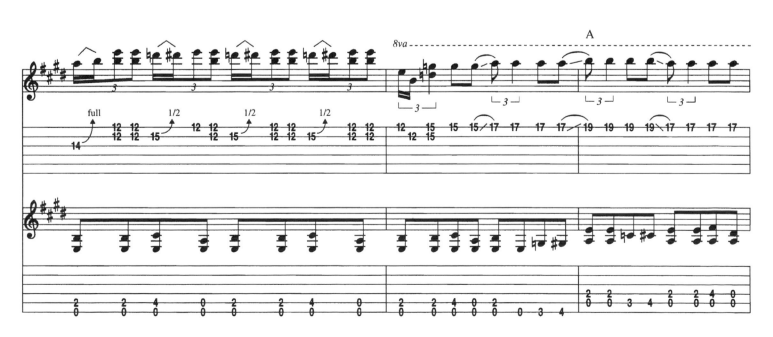

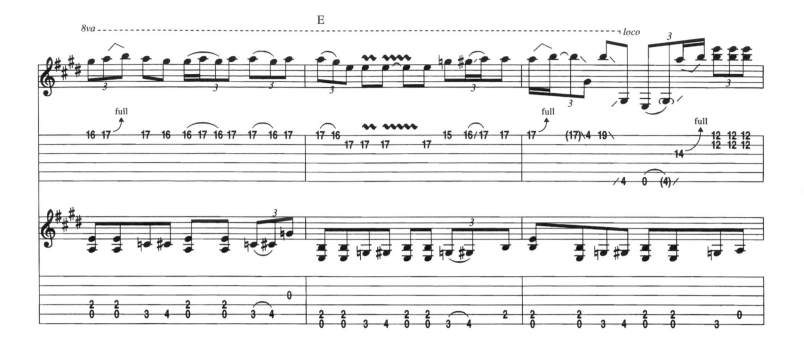

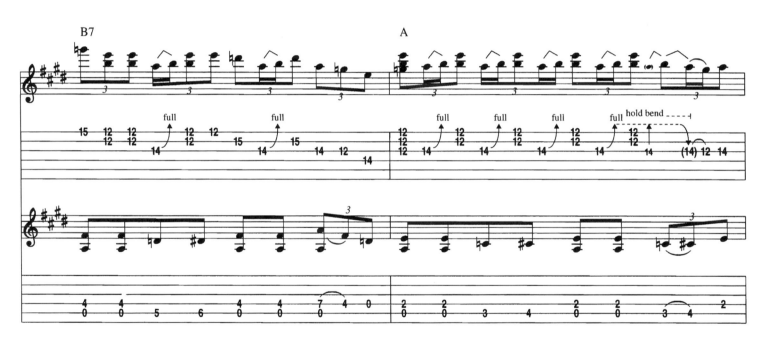

Verse

5. What a-bout the neigh - bors, what they gon-na say? _ Stop lit - tle sis - ter get - ting car-

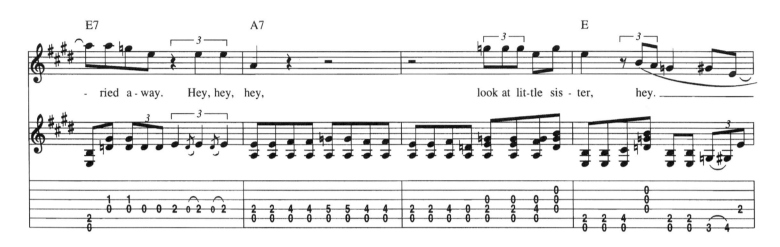

- ried a - way. Hey, hey, hey, look at lit-tle sis - ter, hey. _____

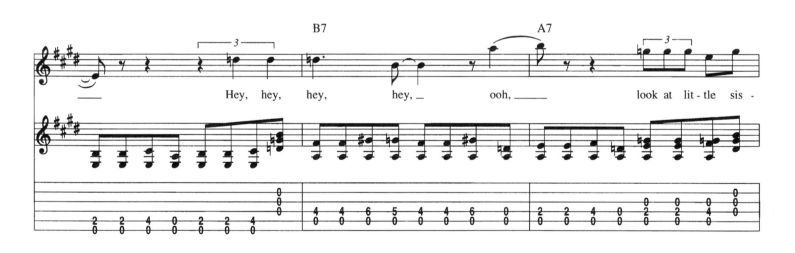

Hey, hey, hey, hey, _ ooh, _____ look at lit - tle sis-

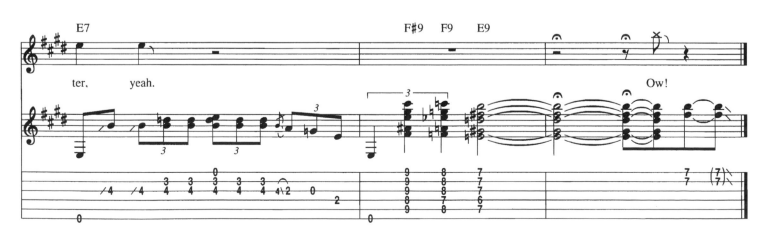

ter, yeah. Ow!

Ain't Gone 'N' Give Up On Love

By Stevie Ray Vaughan

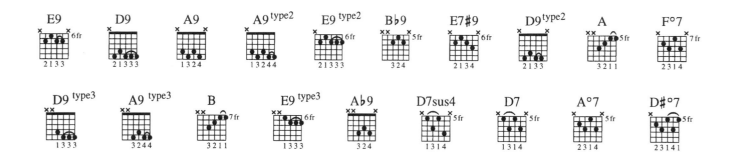

Tune Down 1/2 Step:
①=E♭ ④=D♭
②=B♭ ⑤=A♭
③=G♭ ⑥=E♭

Intro
Slow Blues ♩. = 50

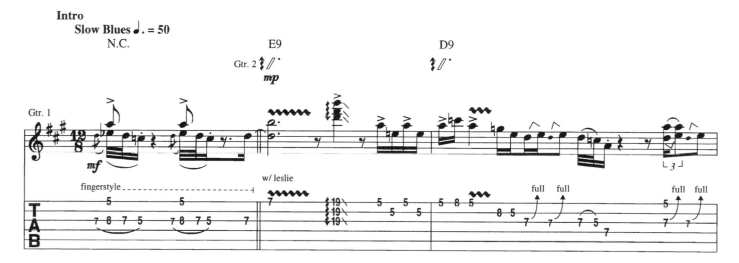

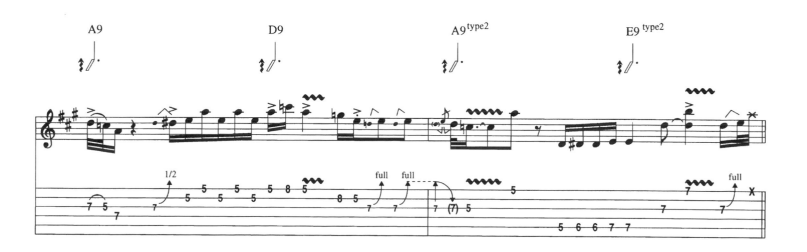

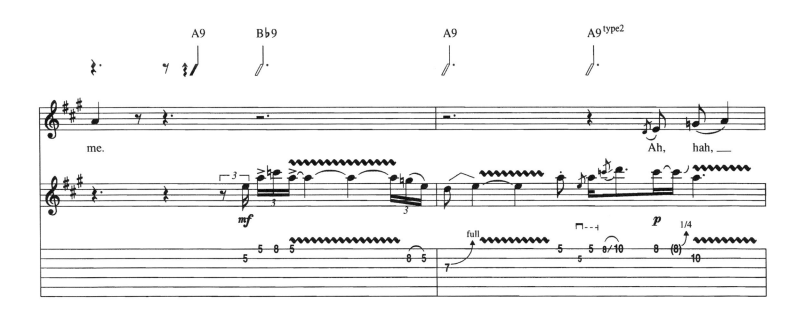

* Organ arr. for gtr.

An' ev-'ry tear that I've cried _____ on - ly washed a-way the fear in - side. _ Now I

I ain't gone 'n' give up on _____ love.

Verse

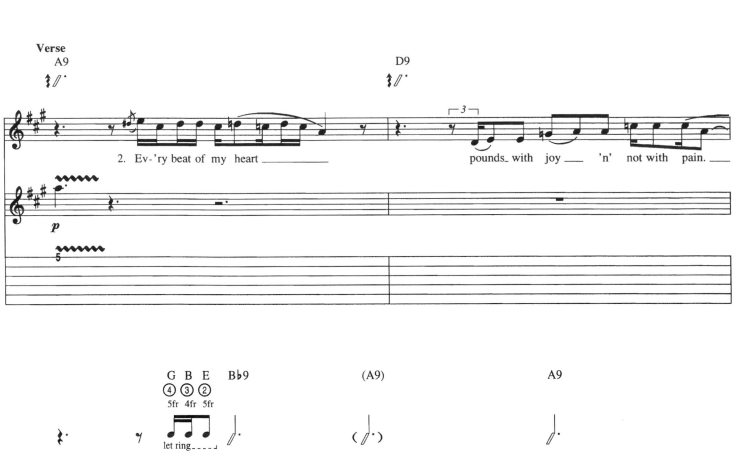

2. Ev-'ry beat of my heart _____ pounds_ with joy _____ 'n' not with pain. _____

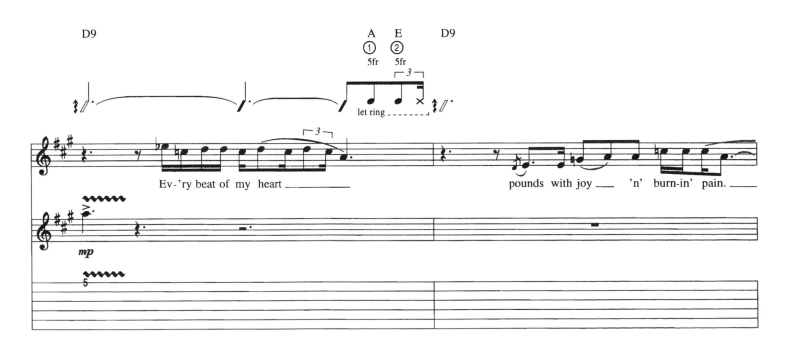

Ev-'ry beat of my heart _____ pounds with joy _____ 'n' burn-in' pain. _____

'Cause all these ah pain - ful mem-o - ries _____ on - ly brought me to my knees. _

I was just giv-in' up on _____ love.

Bridge

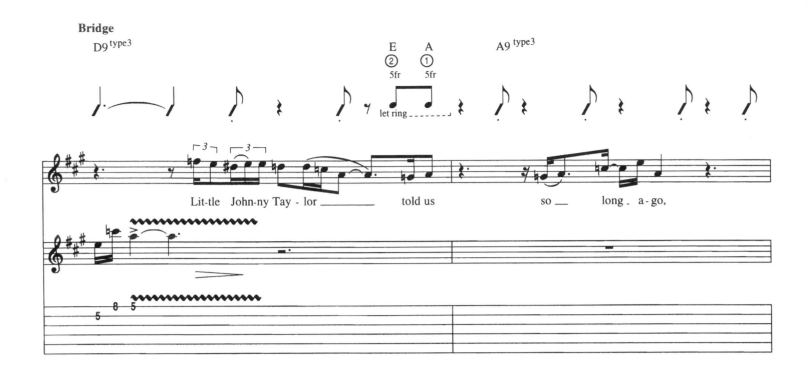

Lit-tle John-ny Tay - lor _____ told us so _____ long _ a-go,

all a-bout_the mid-night cry'n', _ whoa, _ 'n' that you been ly-in'.

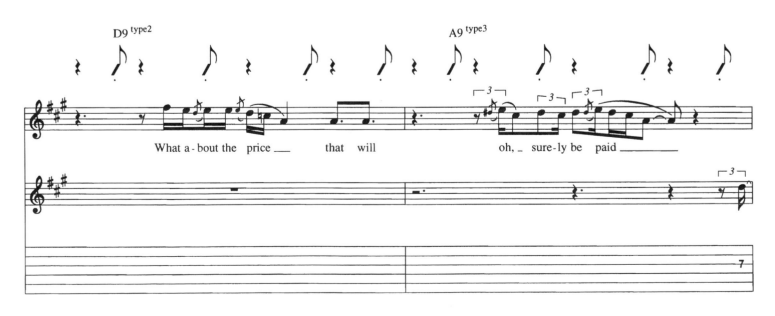

What a-bout the price _____ that will oh, _ sure-ly be paid _____

'cause they gave up on love?   Love   will __ have its day. _____

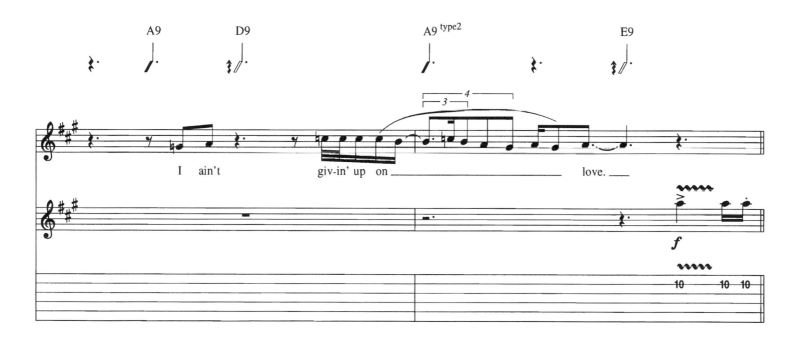

I   ain't   giv-in' up on _____ love. ___

Guitar Solo

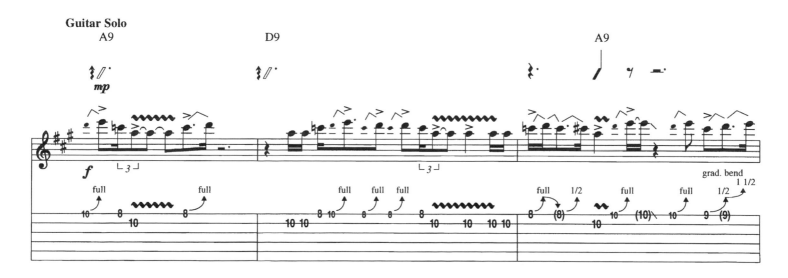

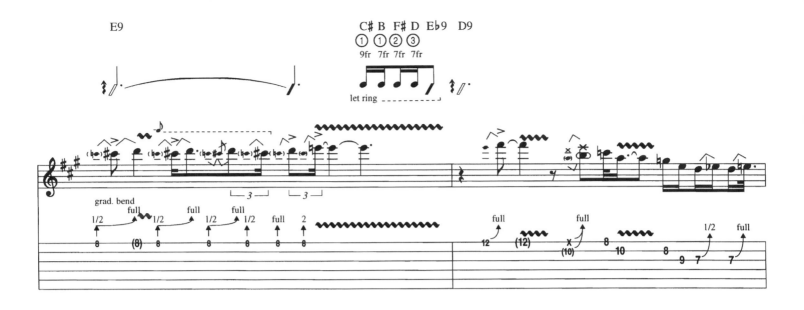

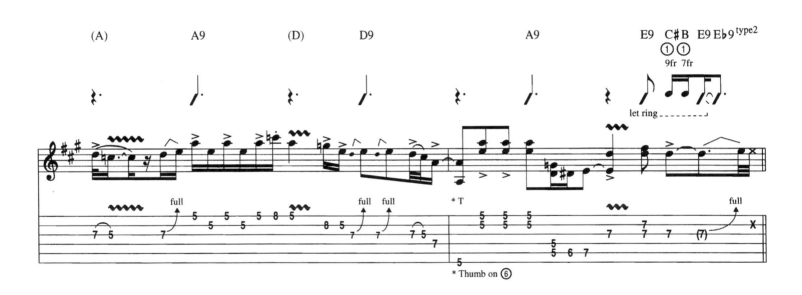

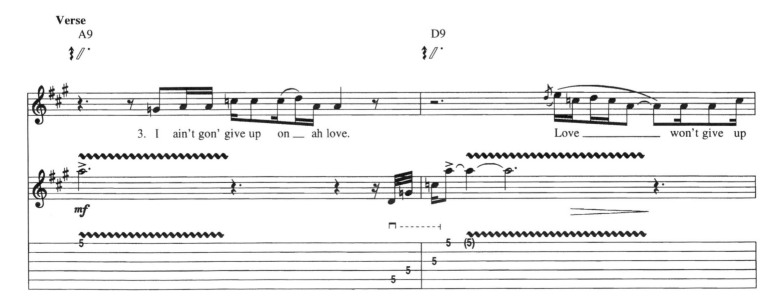

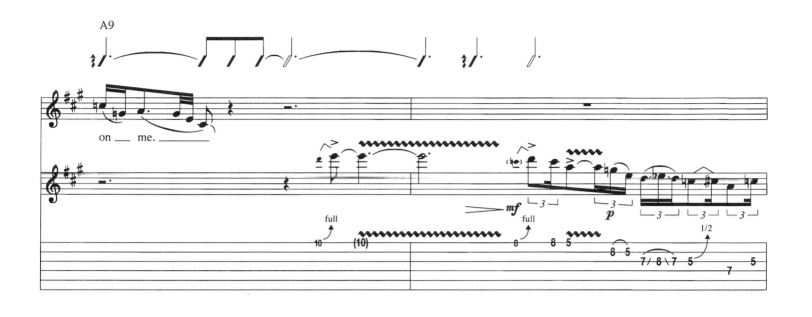

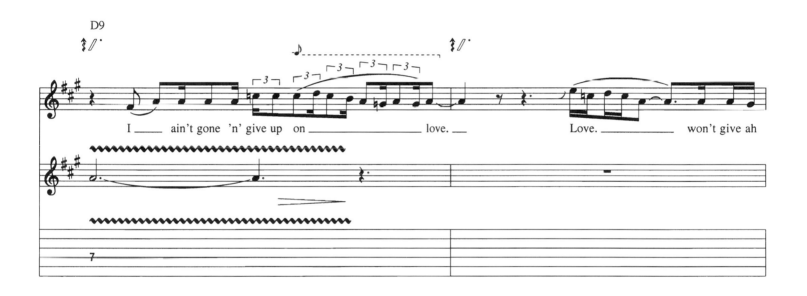

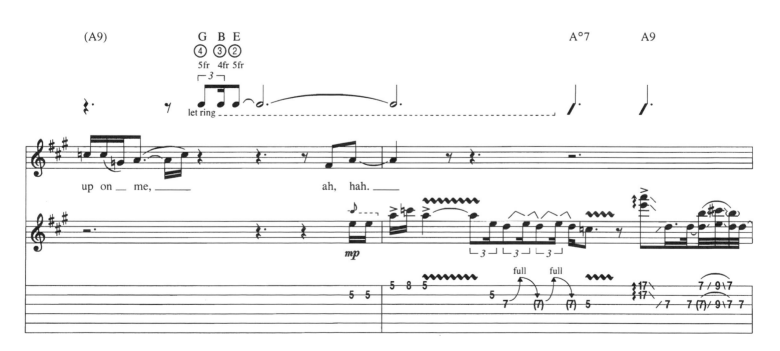

Ev - 'ry time I cry, Lord, just ah won't 'n' let ah me, me be.

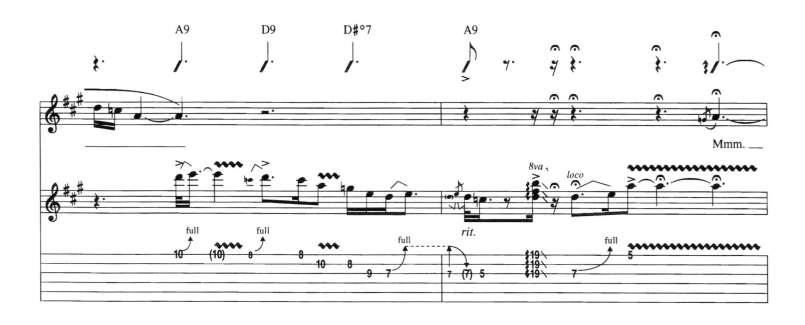

Mmm.

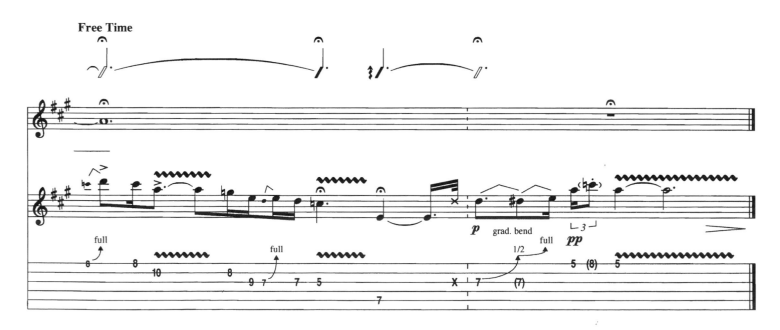

Gone Home

by Eddie Harris

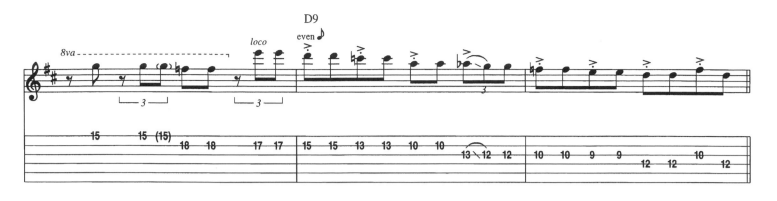

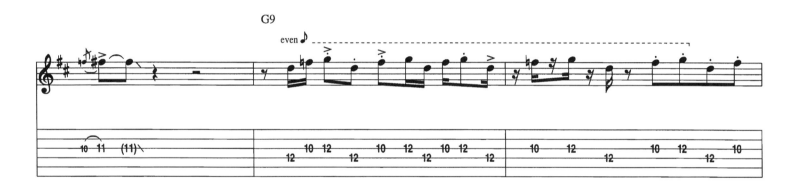

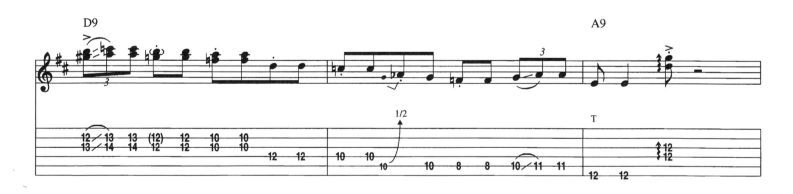

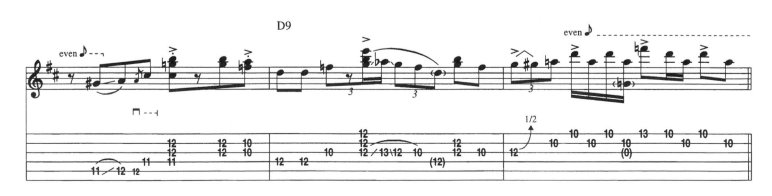

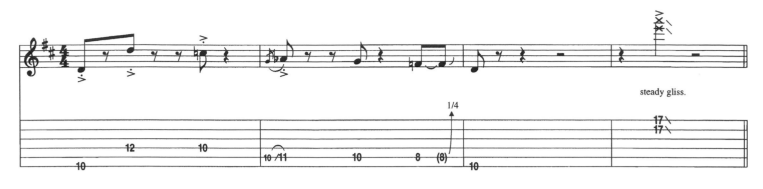

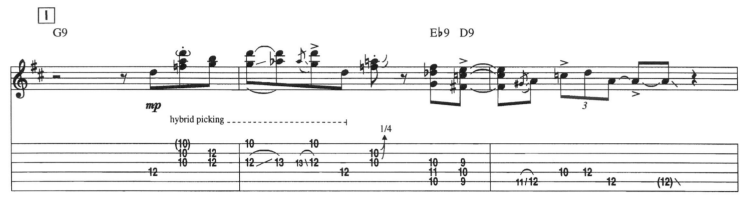

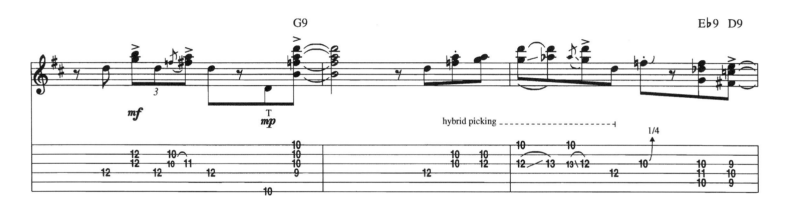

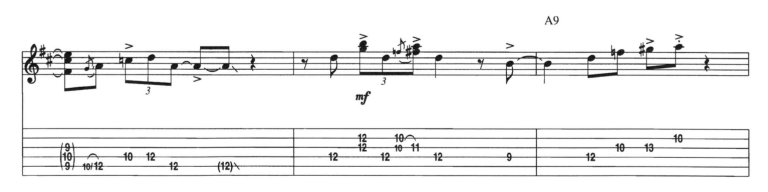

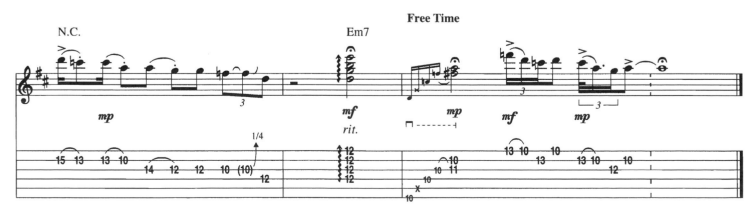

Change It

By Doyle Bramhall

If time is all that we got, then ba-by, let's take
range it. For-get all those pain-ful mem-o-ries, our love's gon-na
passed. last.

To Coda ⊕
Verse

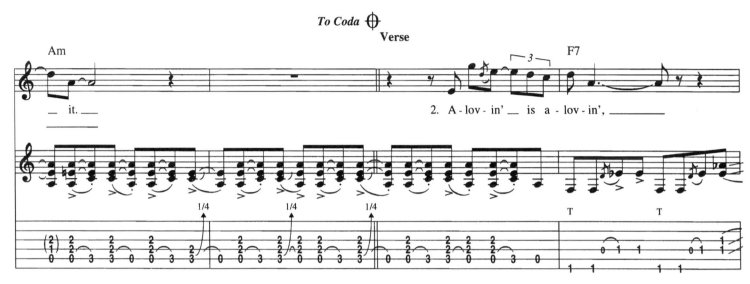

it. 2. A-lov-in' is a-lov-in',

the mo-ment is a-right. It's worth all the years in the past.

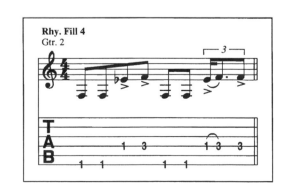

Let's go one more night. _____

Bridge

Get a - way   from the blind _

_ side of   life. _   Hon-ey, I want you to   be __ by   my side.   Me 'n' my back

Gtr. 2: w/ Rhy. Fill 1, 2nd time

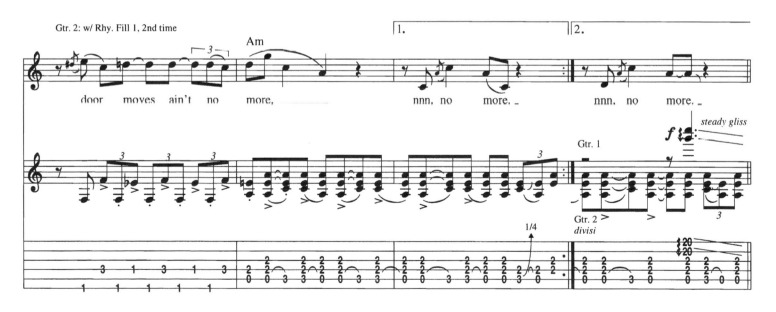

door   moves   ain't   no   more,   nnn, no   more. _   nnn, no   more. _

Rhy. Fill 1
Gtr. 2

Guitar Solo

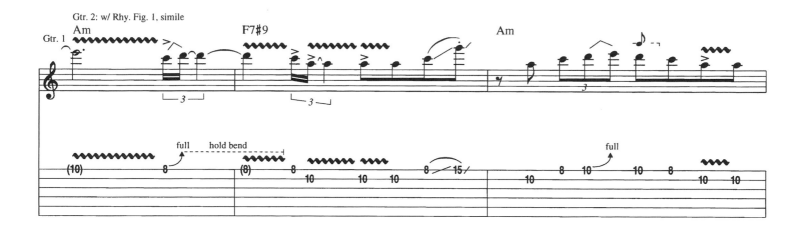

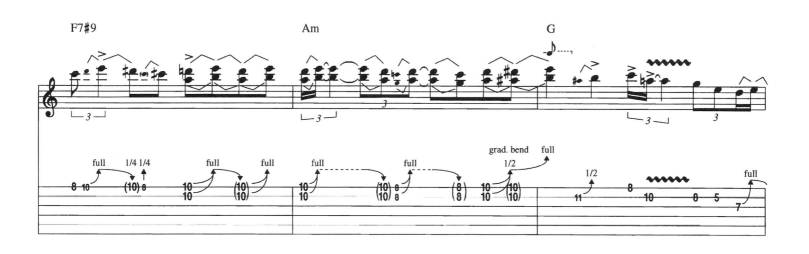

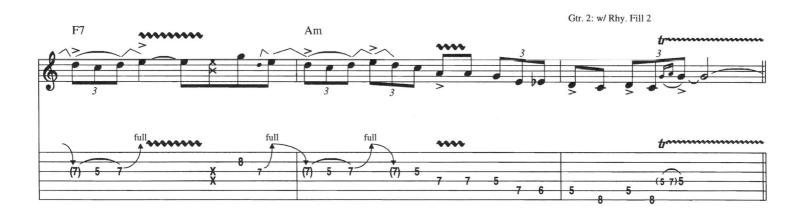

Bridge

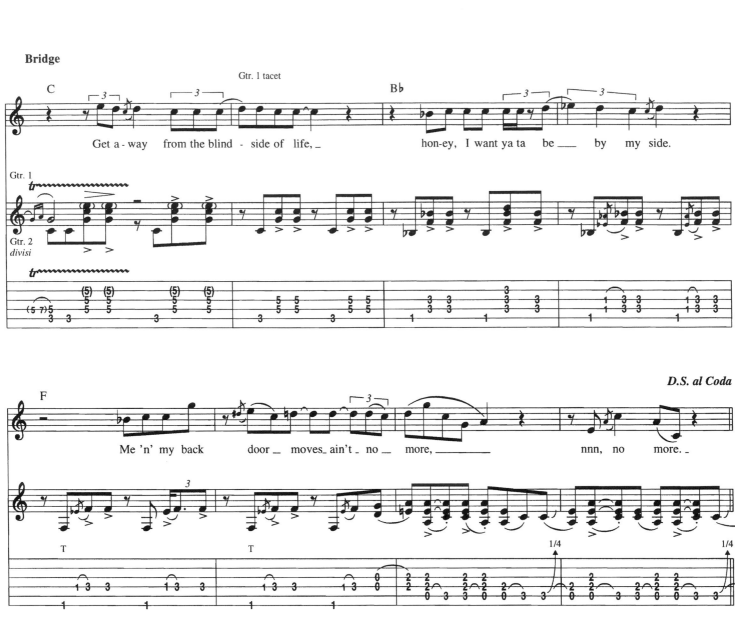

Get a-way from the blind - side of life, __ hon-ey, I want ya ta be __ by my side.

D.S. al Coda

Me 'n' my back door __ moves__ ain't __ no __ more, _____ nnn, no more. __

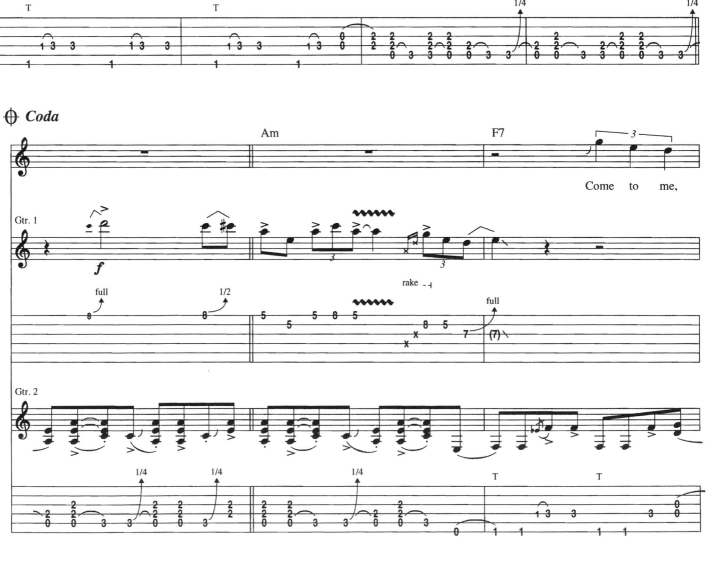

Coda

Come to me,

ba-by,   come to me one ___ more ___ time. ___   It's time we got

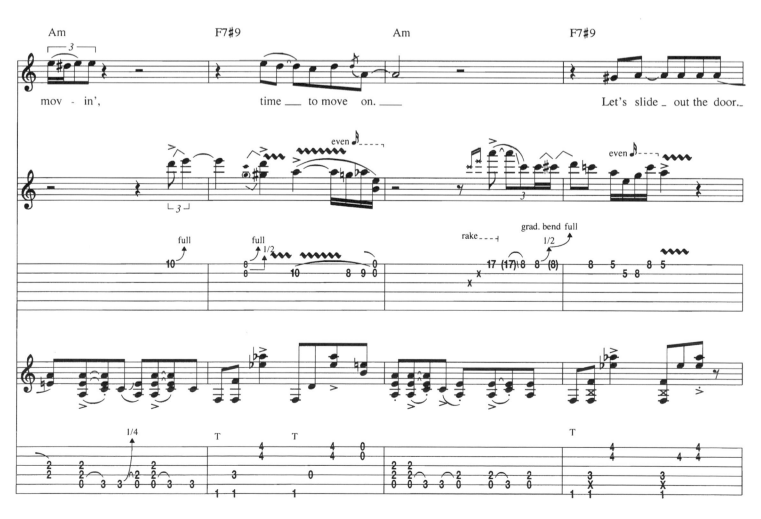

mov - in',   time ___ to move on. ___   Let's slide ___ out the door. ___

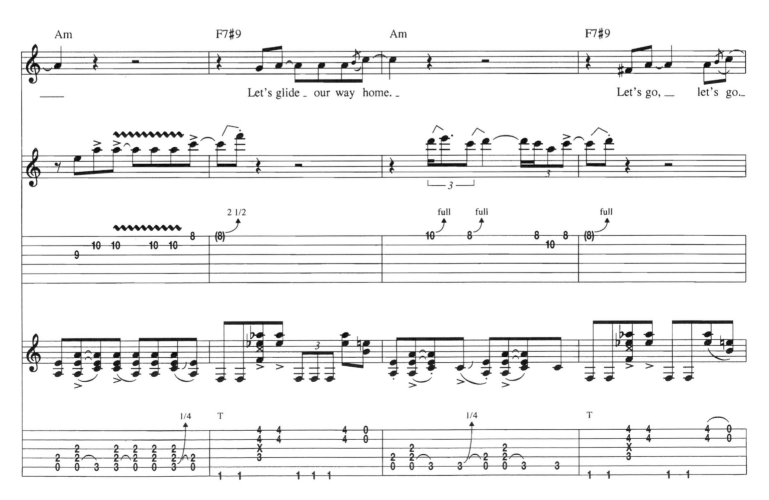

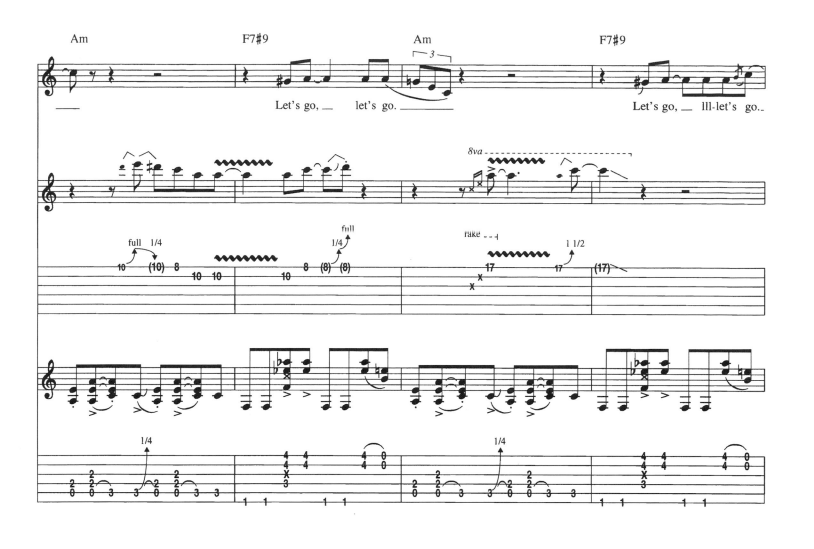

Let's go, — let's go. —
Let's go, — lll-let's go.

I've come. back for mo'.

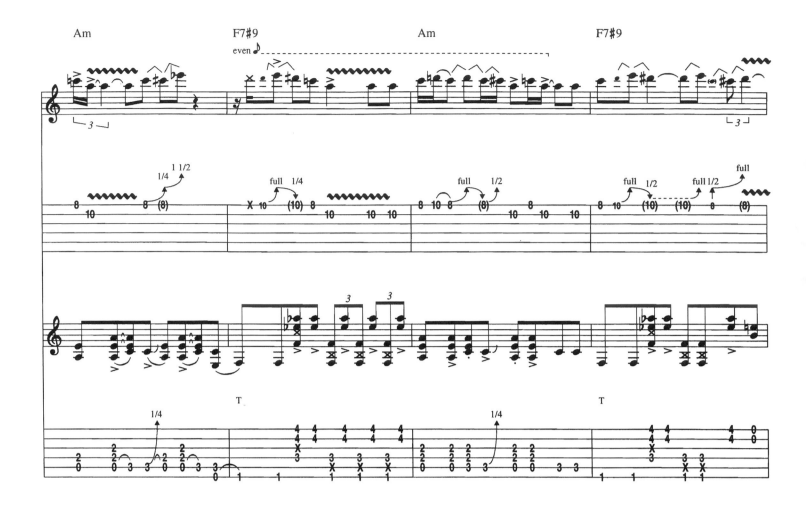

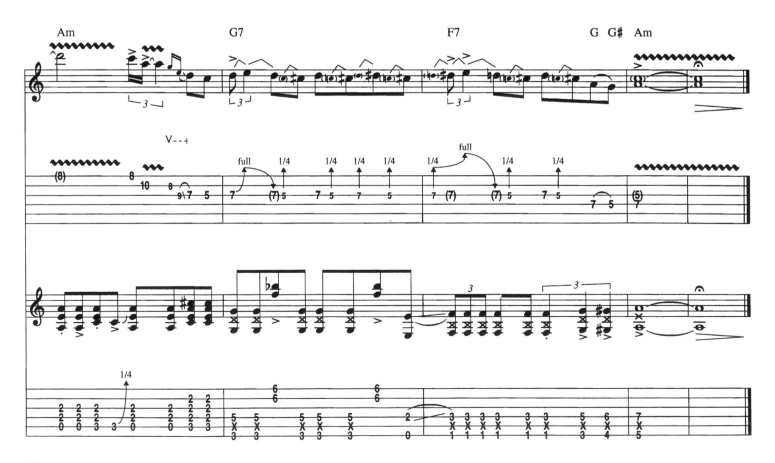

You'll Be Mine

By Willie Dixon

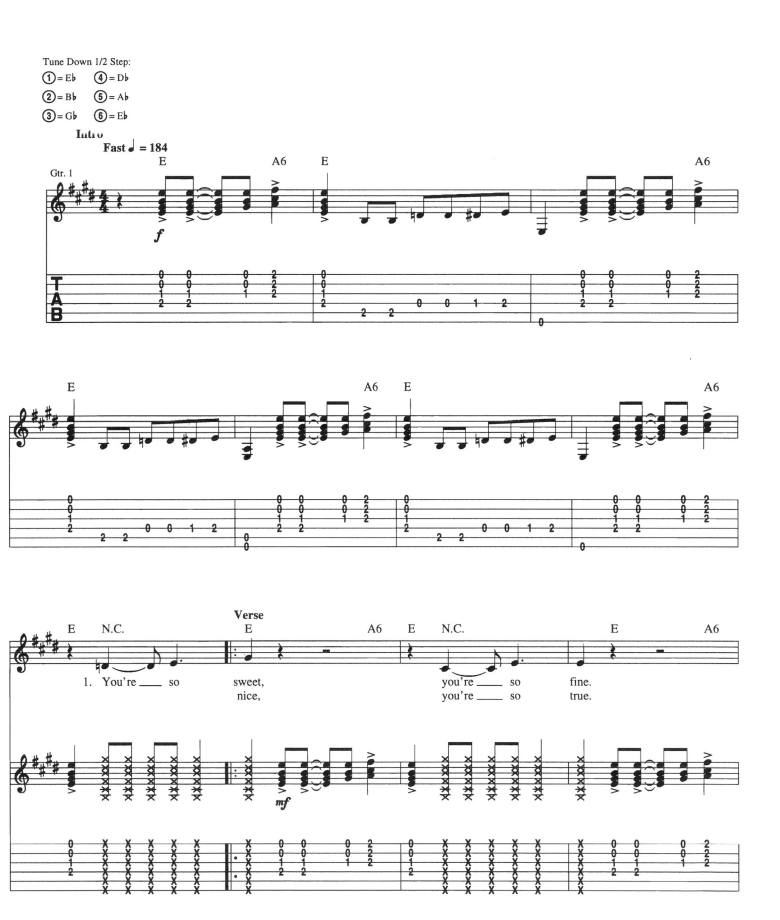

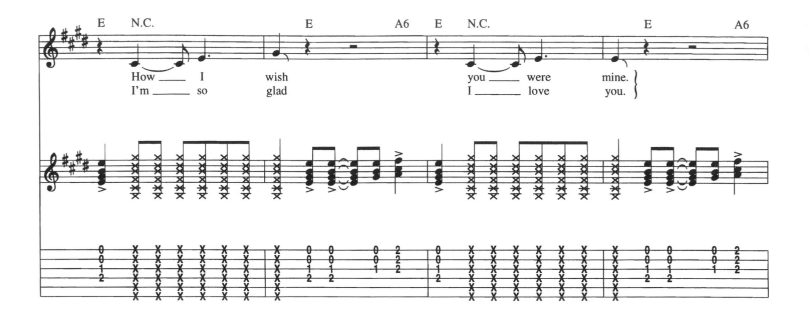

How ____ I wish / I'm ____ so glad ____ you ____ were ____ mine. / I ____ love ____ you.

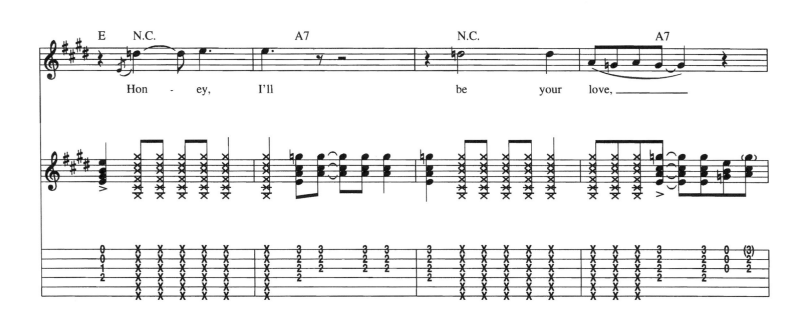

Hon - ey, I'll ____ be your love, ____

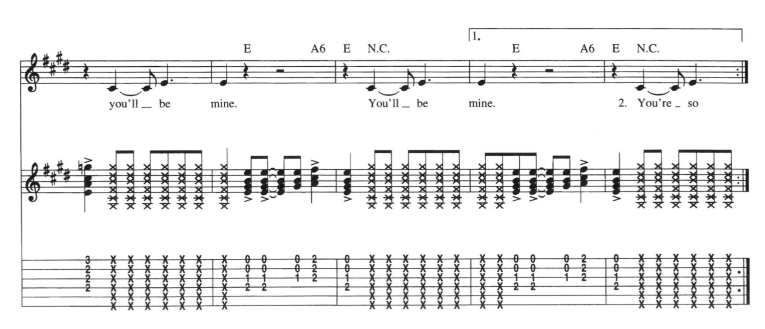

you'll ____ be mine. / You'll ____ be mine. / 2. You're ____ so

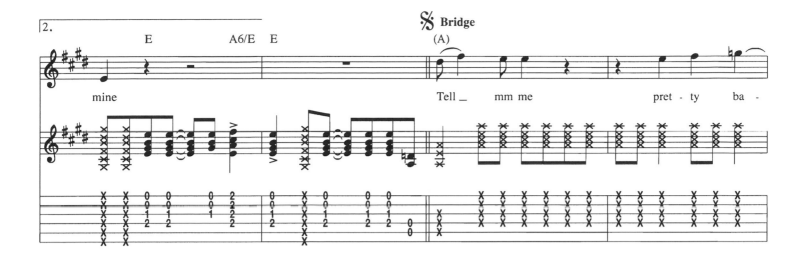

mine

Tell _ mm me pret - ty ba -

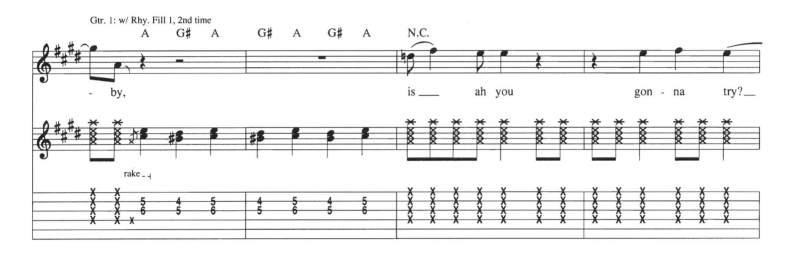

- by, is __ ah you gon - na try? __

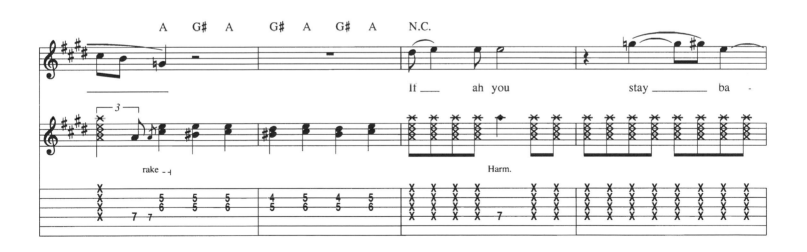

If __ ah you stay _____ ba -

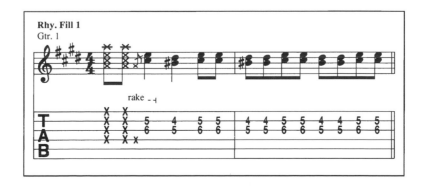

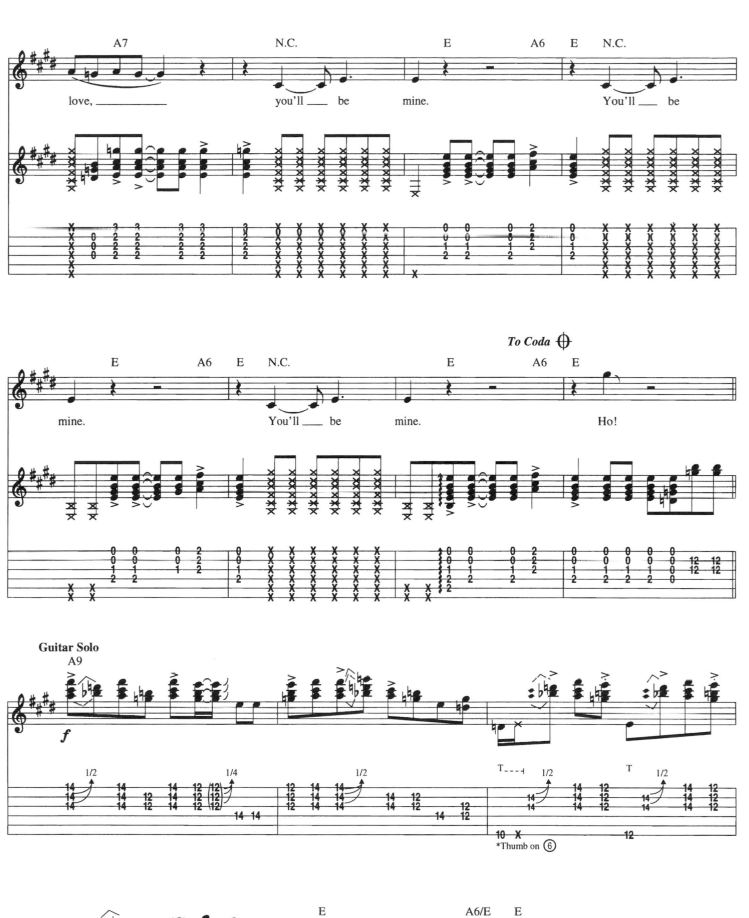

Guitar Solo

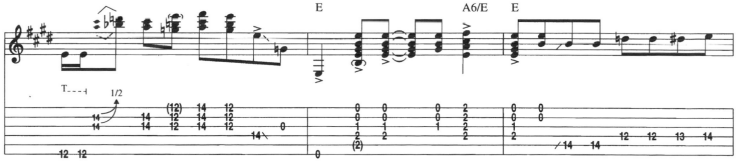

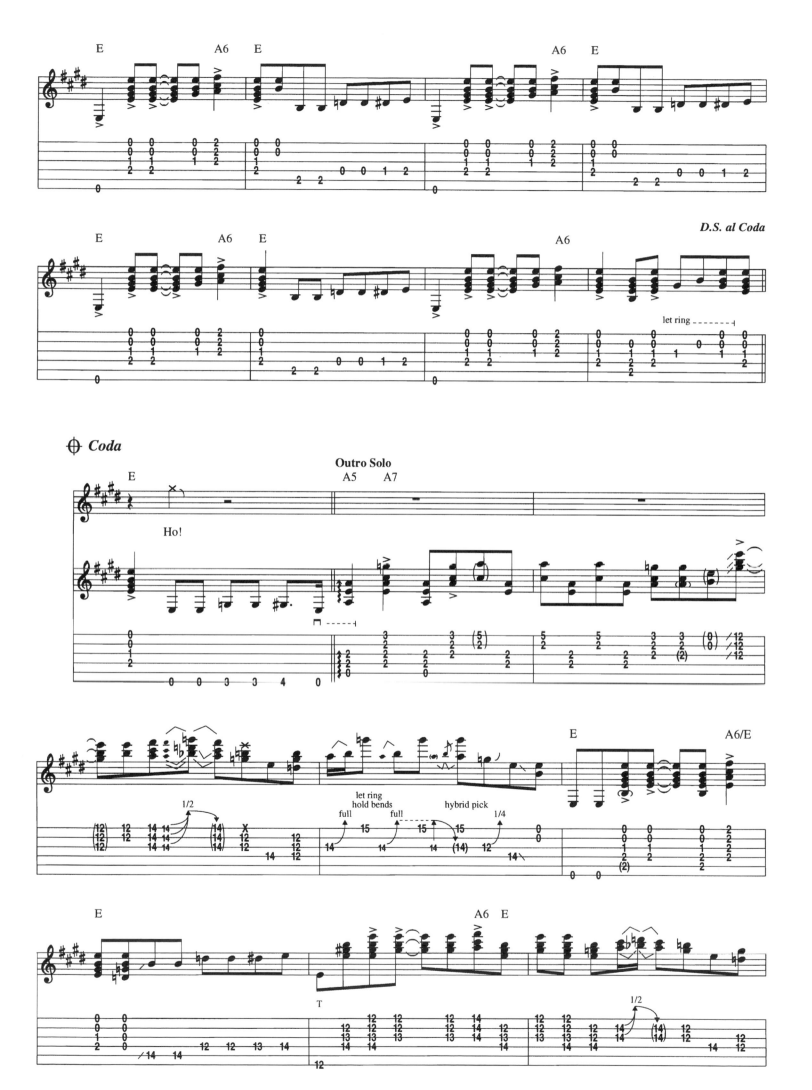

Empty Arms

By Stevie Ray Vaughan

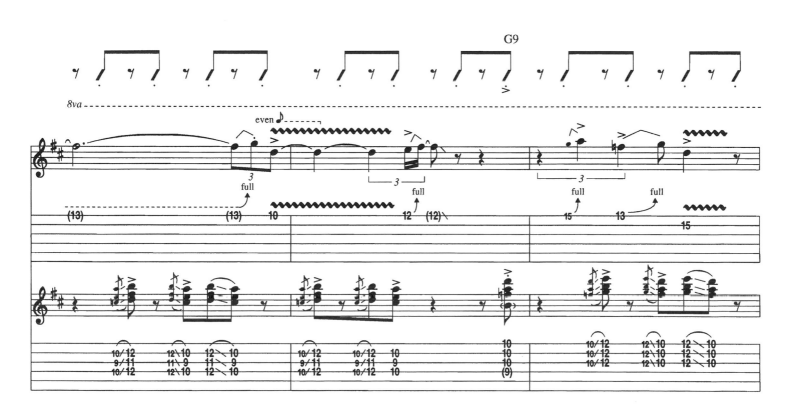

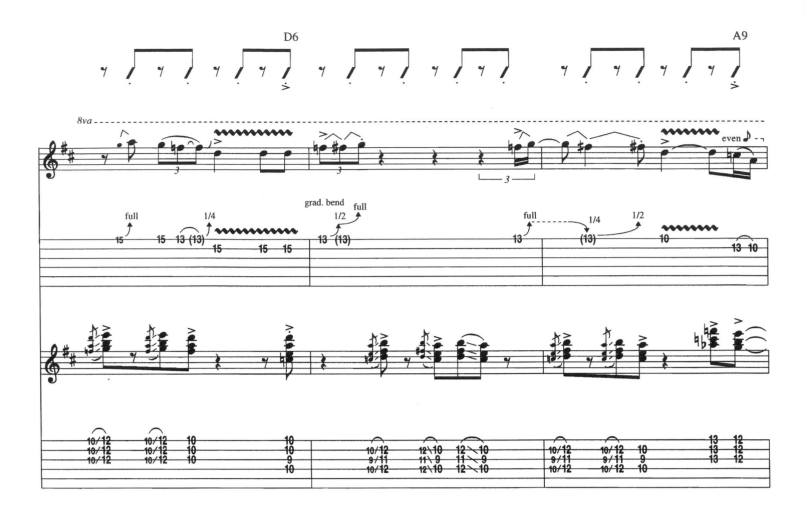

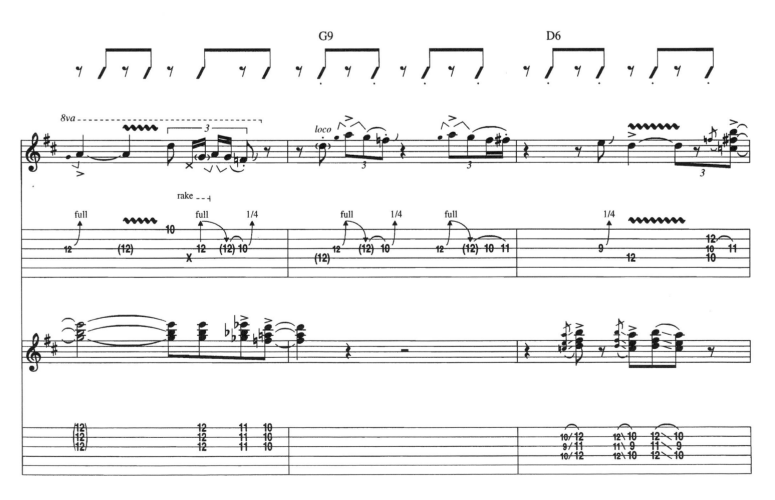

1. You're gon-na miss me _ lit-tle darl - in', the day that I'm gone..

2., 3. *See Additional Lyrics*

**Thumb on ⑥

Gtr. 1: w/ Fill 4, 2nd time

Gtr. 1: w/ Fill 6, 3rd time (see next page)   Gtr. 1: w/ Fill 1, 1st time

You're _ gon-na miss _ me _ lit-tle ba - by,

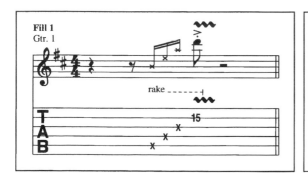

Fill 1
Gtr. 1

rake

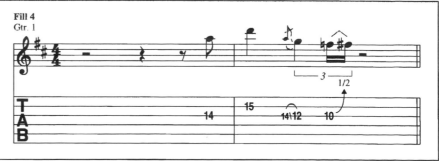

Fill 4
Gtr. 1

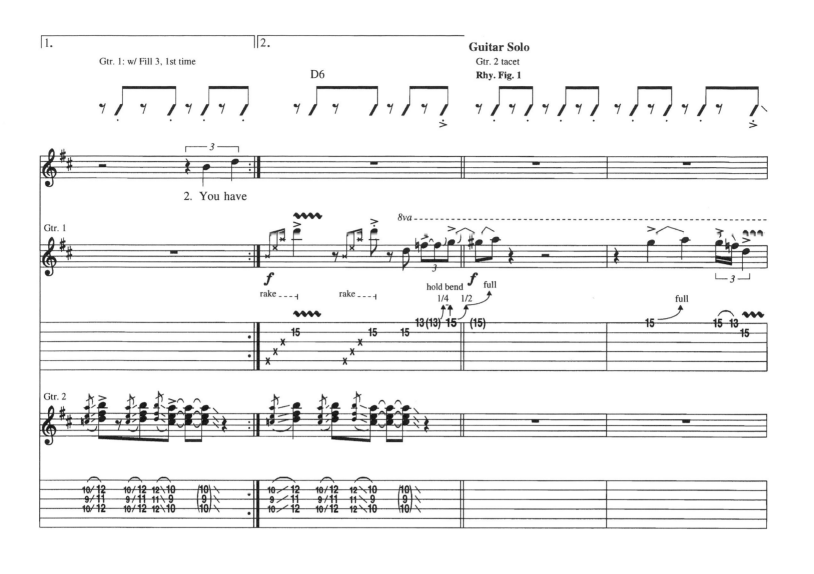

2. You have

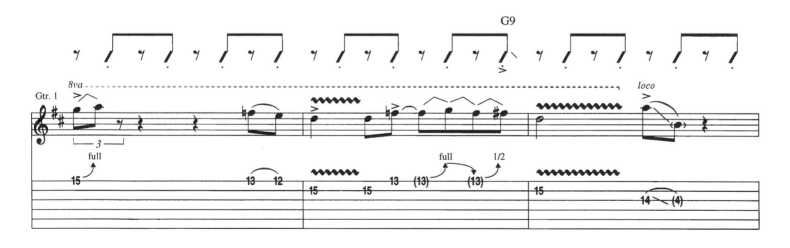

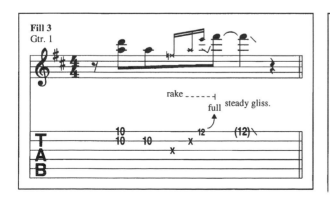

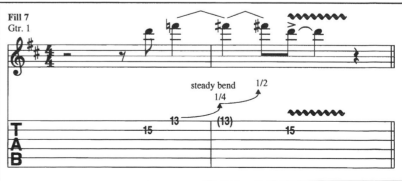

Additional Lyrics

2. You have run me ragged, baby,
   You have run me ragged, baby,
   Your own fault, you're on, your own.
   You didn't want me, no way, baby,
   'Til that other man was gone.
   your own fault, you're own, your own.

3. You can try to get me back baby,
   With all your tricks and charms.
   You can try to get me back baby,
   With all your tricks and charms.
   But when all o' your games are over,
   You'll be left with empty arms.

Come On (Part III)

Words and Music by Earl King

Tune Down 1/2 Step:
①= Eb ④= Db
②= Bb ⑤= Ab
③= Gb ⑥= Eb

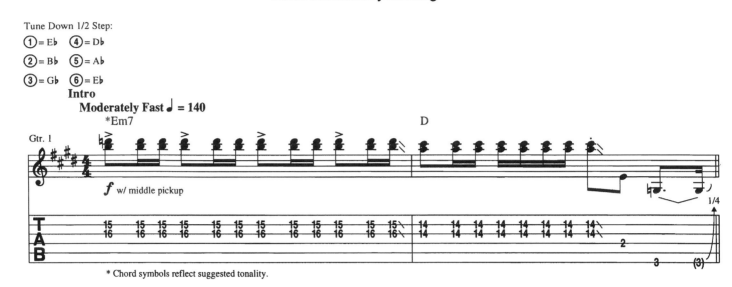

Intro
Moderately Fast ♩ = 140

*Chord symbols reflect suggested tonality.

Verse

Gtr. 1: w/ Rhy. Fill 2, 3rd time

1. Mm, peo-ple talk-in', but they just don't __ know __ what's in my heart and why I
2. A lot of peo-ple liv-in' make be-lieve, __ they keep a lot-ta grit __
3. A love is nice __ if it's un-der-stood. It's ev-en nic-er when you

switch to neck pickup

grad. bend
1/2

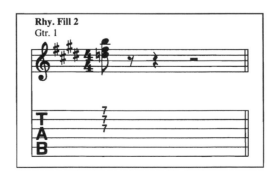

Rhy. Fill 2
Gtr. 1

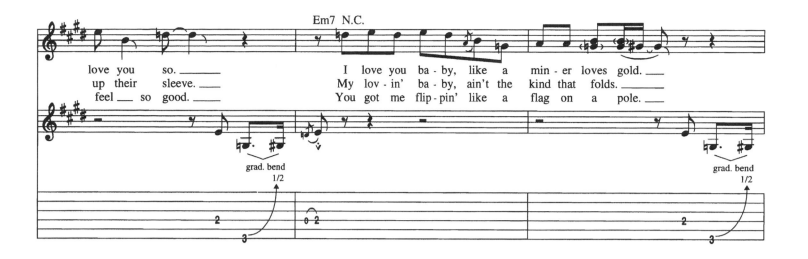

love you so. _____   I love you ba-by, like a min-er loves gold. _____
up their sleeve. _____   My lov-in' ba-by, ain't the kind that folds. _____
feel _____ so good. _____   You got me flip-pin' like a flag on a pole.

Come on _____ ba-by, let the good times ah roll.
Come on _____ ba-by, let the good times ah roll.
Come on _____ sug-ar, let the good times ah roll. _____

Chorus

Ah, let the good times roll. _____
Ah, let the good times roll. _____

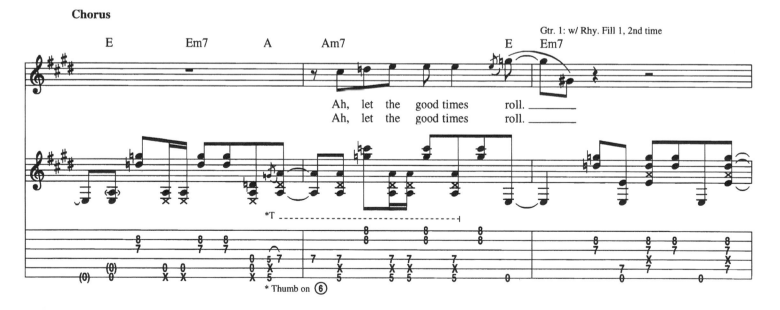

* Thumb on ⑥

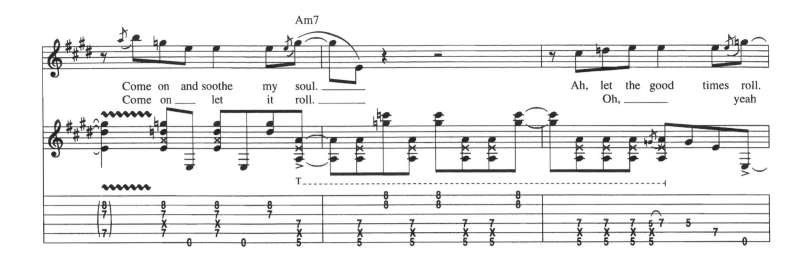

Come on and soothe my soul.
Come on ___ let it roll. ___

Ah, let the good times roll.
Oh, ___ yeah

Gtr. 1: w/ Riff A, 2nd time

Come on, ___
Let it roll. ___

come on, ___
Come on, ___

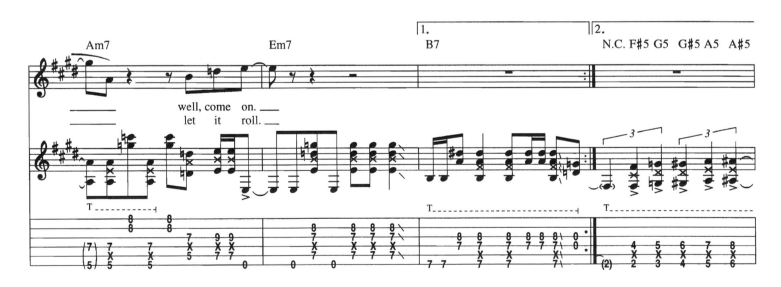

well, come on. ___
let it roll. ___

Riff A
Gtr. 1

D.S. al Coda

⊕ Coda

Chorus

Oh, let the good times roll. ___

Come on 'n' let it roll. ___   Come on, ___ come on. ___

Life Without You

By Stevie Ray Vaughan

Tune Down 1/2 Step:
①= Eb   ④= Db
②= Bb   ⑤= Ab
③= Gb   ⑥= Eb

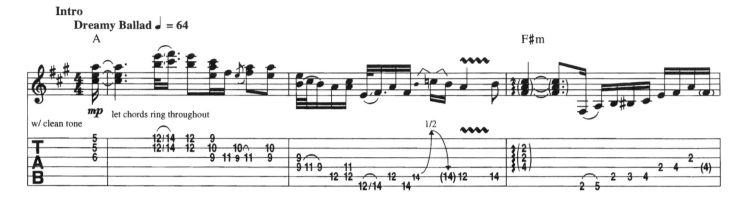

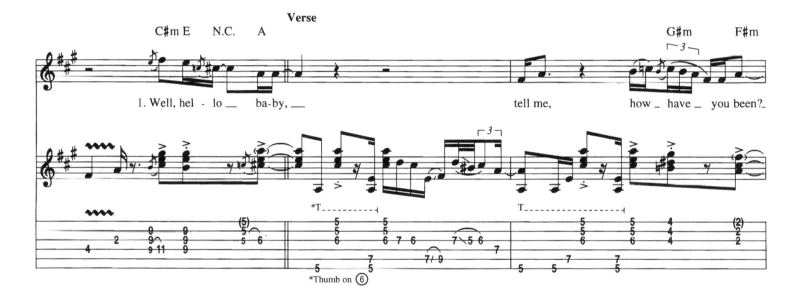

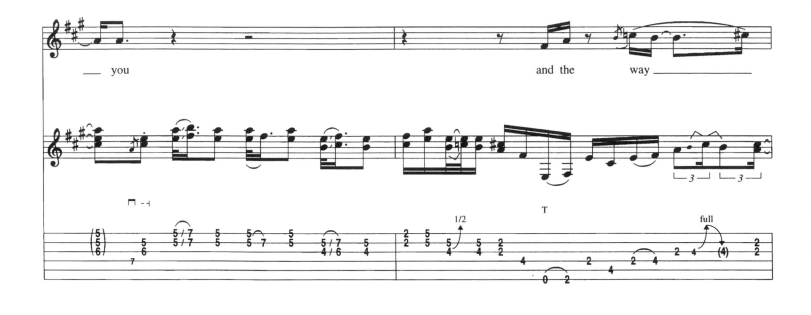

— you

and the way _____

F#m

you grin.

C#mE N.C. A

The day is nec - es-sar - y

B C C#

ev-'ry now __ and then, __

for souls to move __ on, __

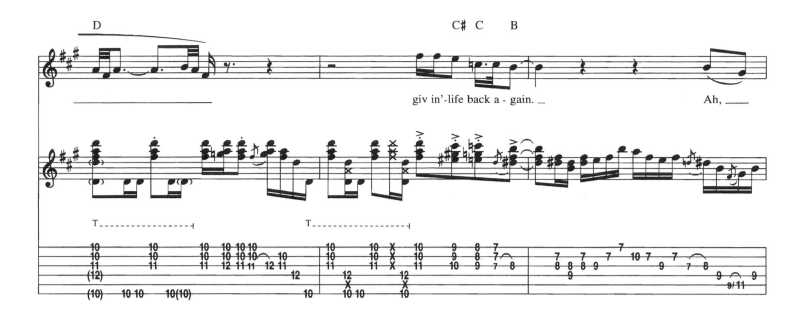

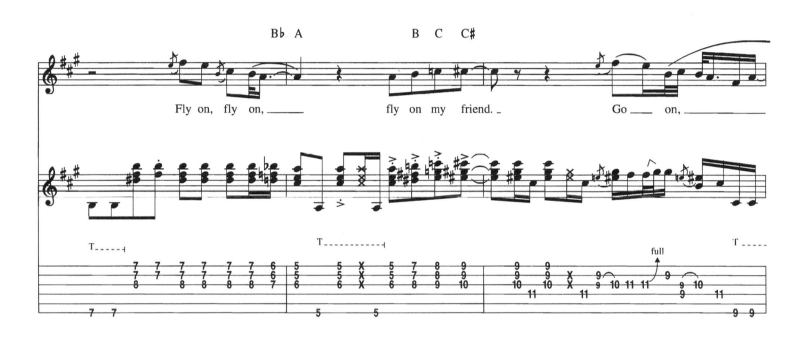

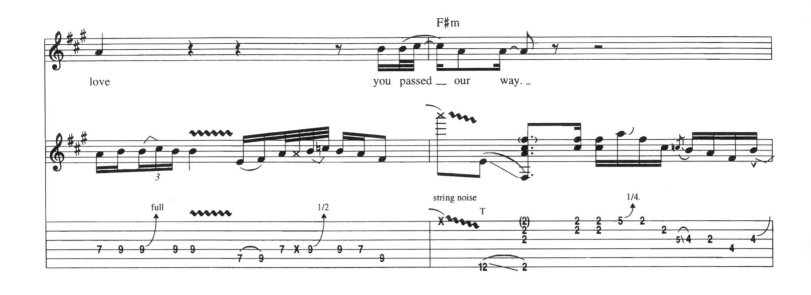

love

F#m

you passed __ our way. _

A

The an - gels have wait - ed _____

for so long. _

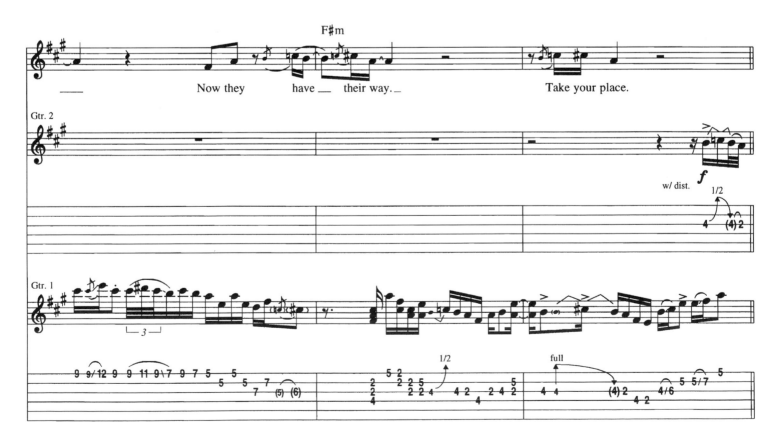

F#m

Now they have __ their way. _

Take your place.

Gtr. 2

w/ dist.

Gtr. 1

Begin Fade

Fade Out

NOTATION LEGEND

GUITAR *signature licks*

Signature Licks book/audio packs provide a step-by-step breakdown of "right from the record" riffs, licks, and solos so you can jam along with your favorite bands. They contain performance notes and an overview of each artist's or group's style, with note-for-note transcriptions in notes and tab. The online audio tracks feature full-band demos at both normal and slow speeds.

AC/DC
14041352......................$24.99

AEROSMITH 1973-1979
00695106......................$24.99

AEROSMITH 1979-1998
00695219 .... $22.95

DUANE ALLMAN
00696042......................$24.99

BEST OF CHET ATKINS
00695752......................$24.99

AVENGED SEVENFOLD
00696473......................$24.99

THE BEATLES
00298845......................$24.99

BEST OF THE BEATLES FOR ACOUSTIC GUITAR
00695453......................$24.99

THE BEATLES HITS
00695049......................$24.95

JEFF BECK
00696427......................$24.99

BEST OF GEORGE BENSON
00695418......................$22.99

BEST OF BLACK SABBATH
00695249......................$24.99

BLUES BREAKERS WITH JOHN MAYALL & ERIC CLAPTON
00696374......................$24.99

BON JOVI
00696380.................. $22.99

ROY BUCHANAN
00696654.................. $22.99

KENNY BURRELL
00695830......................$27.99

BEST OF CHARLIE CHRISTIAN
00695584......................$24.99

BEST OF ERIC CLAPTON
00695038......................$24.99

ERIC CLAPTON – FROM THE ALBUM UNPLUGGED
00695250......................$24.99

BEST OF CREAM
00695251......................$24.99

THE DOORS
00695373 .... $22.95

DEEP PURPLE – GREATEST HITS
00695625......................$24.99

DREAM THEATER
00111943......................$24.99

TOMMY EMMANUEL
00696409..................... $22.99

ESSENTIAL JAZZ GUITAR
00695875..................... $19.99

FLEETWOOD MAC
00696416 .... $22.99

ROBBEN FORD
00695903...................... $22.95

BEST OF GRANT GREEN
00695747......................$24.99

PETER GREEN
00145386......................$24.99

BEST OF GUNS N' ROSES
00695183......................$24.99

THE BEST OF BUDDY GUY
00695186 .... $22.99

JIM HALL
00695848 ....$29.99

JIMI HENDRIX
00696560......................$24.99

JIMI HENDRIX – VOLUME 2
00695835 ....$24.99

JOHN LEE HOOKER
00695894......................$24.99

BEST OF JAZZ GUITAR
00695586......................$29.99

ERIC JOHNSON
00699317......................$24.99

ROBERT JOHNSON
00695264......................$24.99

BARNEY KESSEL
00696009......................$24.99

THE ESSENTIAL ALBERT KING
00695713......................$24.99

B.B. KING – BLUES LEGEND
00696039......................$22.99

B.B. KING – THE DEFINITIVE COLLECTION
00695635......................$22.99

MARK KNOPFLER
00695178......................$24.99

LYNYRD SKYNYRD
00695872......................$24.99

THE BEST OF YNGWIE MALMSTEEN
00695669......................$24.99

BEST OF PAT MARTINO
00695632......................$24.99

MEGADETH
00696421......................$22.99

WES MONTGOMERY
00695387......................$24.99

BEST OF NIRVANA
00695483......................$24.95

VERY BEST OF OZZY OSBOURNE
00695431 .... $22.99

BRAD PAISLEY
00696379......................$22.99

BEST OF JOE PASS
00695730......................$24.99

TOM PETTY
00696021......................$24.99

PINK FLOYD
00103659......................$27.99

THE GUITARS OF ELVIS
00174800......................$22.99

BEST OF QUEEN
00695097......................$24.99

RADIOHEAD
00109304......................$24.99

BEST OF RAGE AGAINST THE MACHINE
00695480......................$24.99

JERRY REED
00118236 ....$22.99

BEST OF DJANGO REINHARDT
00695660......................$27.99

BEST OF ROCK 'N' ROLL GUITAR
00695559......................$24.99

BEST OF ROCKABILLY GUITAR
00695785......................$22.99

BEST OF CARLOS SANTANA
00174664......................$22.99

BEST OF JOE SATRIANI
00695216 ....$24.99

SLASH
00696576......................$22.99

SLAYER
00121281......................$22.99

BEST OF SOUTHERN ROCK
00695560......................$19.95

STEELY DAN
00696015......................$22.99

MIKE STERN
00695800......................$27.99

BEST OF SURF GUITAR
00695822......................$22.99

STEVE VAI
00673247......................$24.99

STEVE VAI – ALIEN LOVE SECRETS: THE NAKED VAMPS
00695223......................$27.99

STEVE VAI – FIRE GARDEN: THE NAKED VAMPS
00695166......................$22.95

STEVE VAI – THE ULTRA ZONE: NAKED VAMPS
00695684......................$22.95

VAN HALEN
00110227......................$27.99

THE GUITAR STYLE OF STEVIE RAY VAUGHAN
00695155......................$24.95

BEST OF THE VENTURES
00695772......................$24.99

THE WHO – 2ND ED.
00695561 ....$22.95

JOHNNY WINTER
00695951 ....$24.99

YES
00113120......................$24.99

NEIL YOUNG – GREATEST HITS
00695988......................$24.99

BEST OF ZZ TOP
00695738......................$24.99

HAL•LEONARD®

www.halleonard.com

COMPLETE DESCRIPTIONS AND SONGLISTS ONLINE!

Prices, contents and availability subject to change without notice.